D1174248

The Day of the Disaster

WACO CULT INFERNO

April 19, 1993

Written By Sue L. Hamilton

NOTE: The following is a fictional account based on factual data.

Published by Abdo & Daughters, 4940 Viking Drive, Suite 622, Edina, MN 55435.

Library bound edition distributed by Rockbottom Books, Pentagon Tower, P.O. Box 36036, Minneapolis, Minnesota 55435.

Cover Photo by: AP/Wide World Photos.
Inside Photos by: AP/Wide World Photos (5, 6, 9, 13, 17, 23, 29, 31).
The Bettmann Archive (11, 21, 30).

Edited By: John C. Hamilton

Library of Congress Cataloging–in–Publication Data
Smith, Richard, 1954—
Waco cult inferno / written by Richard Smith.
p. cm — (Day of the disaster)
Includes index.
Summary: Chronicles the events in Waco, Texas, leading up to the fire that killed over ninety members of David Koresh's Branch Davidian cult.
ISBN 1-56239-260-3
1. Waco Branch Davidian Disaster, Tex., 1993—Juvenile literature. 2. Koresh, David, 1960-1993—Juvenile literature. 3. Branch Davidians-Juvenile literature. [1. Waco Branch Davidian Disaster, Tex., 1993. 2. Koresh, David. 3. Branch Davidians.] I. Title. II. Series.
BP605.B72S55 1993
976.4' 284063—dc20

93-5154
CIP
AC

Contents

Prologue
WACO CULT INFERNO

TUESDAY, APRIL 19, 1993
12:01 p.m.

It's going down! Even cult leader David Koresh can't stop the armed power of a U.S. Army tank—its battering ram is splintering the thick wooden walls of his fortress. As I stand here, outside Waco, Texas, it appears Koresh and his Branch Davidians are finally facing the steely arms of justice. After nearly two months in hiding, Koresh will have to answer to the charges of possessing illegal firearms, as well as the cold-blooded murder of four federal agents. It's hard to believe that it's been over 7 weeks since four ATF men died under the cult leader's murderous response to their statement, "You're under arrest..."

12:05 p.m.

Something's not right! Searing waves of flame and blackened clouds of smoke are filling the fortress! I can't see much anymore. At this rate, it'll take only minutes for the fire to engulf the entire compound...and everyone inside it. Is it possible that the cult members have set this fire to kill themselves, rather than be taken to jail? And what about the children? Would he really let the kids die, too?

* * * * *

This is the taped journal of a fictional Alcohol, Tobacco, & Firearms (ATF) officer, witnessing the tragic efforts of local and national law enforcement officials to arrest Branch Davidian cult leader David Koresh.

Officers from The Bureau of Alcohol, Tobacco and Firearms (ATF) enforce laws that have to do with guns and explosives, as well as alcohol and tobacco products. In recent years firearms have become a serious problem in our society. We have laws that say what kinds of guns we may own and how they may be used. Many people, however, are not interested in obeying these laws, and use their guns to rob or kill other people. The ATF's job is to track down people who sell and use guns illegally.

FORWARD

1929

The Branch Davidians are formed by Victor Houteff. They are a religious cult that broke away from a group that earlier had left the Seventh-day Adventists.

1960

Vernon Howell is born in Houston, Texas. He will change his name to David Koresh in 1990.

1974

Rather than continue his education, Koresh drops out of school in the 9th grade. The young 14-year-old spends his time playing the guitar and reading the Bible.

1979

Koresh is baptized into the Seventh-day Adventist Church.

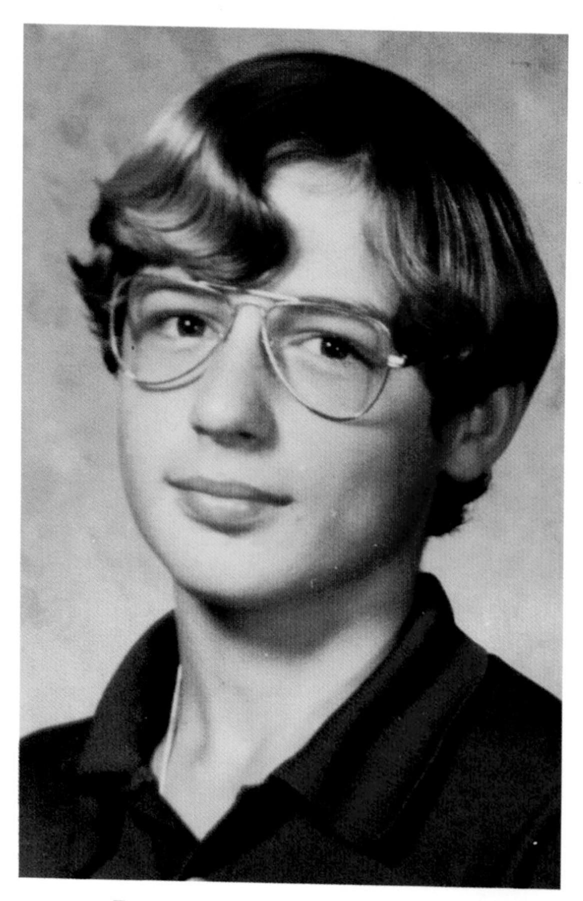

David Koresh at age 14.

1981

Koresh is thrown out of the Adventists because he cannot behave in church. He is soon drawn to the Branch Davidian cult. They welcome him as he is. The cult members live on a farm 10 miles north of Waco, Texas. The name of their compound is Mount Carmel (which is also the name of a place mentioned in the Bible where fire came down from the sky and destroyed the altar of a false god).

Koresh's first "job" at Mount Carmel is as helper to the elderly female leader of the Branch Davidians, Lois Roden.

1983

Lois Roden steps down. Her son, George Roden, takes over as cult leader. Koresh hates that George is now in charge. Koresh works to undermine the man's authority. He wants to become the leader, himself.

1986

Koresh predicts he will die in a bloody battle.

1987

Koresh carries a silver automatic pistol with him wherever he goes. Seeing his chance, he uses the gun to ambush George Roden. The cult leader is badly wounded, but he lives. Police arrest Koresh for attempted murder. During his trial, the jury cannot agree on whether there is enough evidence to convict Koresh. The 27-year old goes free.

1988

Koresh travels to Hawaii, Canada, England and Australia, telling people about his religious beliefs. He wears long, white flowing robes and claims he is God. Many people listen and believe him.

The things Koresh teaches are very strange. He tells the cult members that he is entitled to 140 wives. Not yet 30 years old, Koresh says that he alone knows what is best for people.

SUMMER 1991

The people who believe in Koresh now number in the hundreds. Among them are many children. The size of his following gives him enough power to easily take full control of the Branch Davidians and Mount Carmel.

The followers do everything they can to please Koresh. Believing that the end of the world is coming, he orders them to begin turning Mount Carmel into a fortress. He wants a concrete bunker built in the center of the fortress. Above the bunker he has the people build a tall tower so guards can keep a watchful eye for unwelcome strangers.

Koresh also orders his followers to buy guns—powerful weapons used in warfare. Although many of the guns are bought legally, many are altered so that they can fire shot after shot without lifting a finger off the trigger (an "automatic"). Such weapons are against the law for civilians to own.

This photo, taken approximately six years before the Waco tragedy, shows David Koresh with his wife Rachel and infant son Cyrus.

ATF OFFICIAL'S TAPED JOURNAL
SPRING 1992

JUNE 1992
Houston, Texas

My assignment: follow-up on cult activity in Texas. Word on the street is that David Koresh and his Branch Davidians are stock-piling quite a collection of weapons. It could be he's preparing for something big.

We've got rumors floating around here that the Branch Davidians recently spent $200,000 on weapons and are hiding them inside the fortress. We've got an undercover agent going in this week.

JULY 1992

Our agent's report is in. The cult members do indeed have quite an arsenal of weapons. Next assignment is to find out what they're planning to do with all that firepower.

AUGUST 1992

Koresh is preparing his followers for "the world to end." It sounds like he's planning an attack. On whom, is the question. Whatever his plans, it's our job to stop him before he can hurt or kill even one innocent person.

DECEMBER 1992
Somewhere in Arkansas

Using information supplied by our inside agent, we've built a full-size copy of Koresh's fortress here at our training base. Now is the time for us to train for our attack on Mount Carmel. To protect those inside the complex, we've got to know every door, window, corridor and room in the place. Maybe we can capture Koresh without hurting anyone.

The north side view of David Koresh's cult compound.

The Mount Carmel Assault

SATURDAY, FEBRUARY 27, 1993
Waco, Texas

A leak. The *Waco Tribune-Herald* newspaper got wind of the illegal guns at Mount Carmel. The paper reported that the 135 Branch Davidians living inside the fortress are armed with AK-47 and AR-15 assault rifles.

Naturally, the people of Waco are more than a little upset with this piece of information. A little knowledge can be a dangerous thing. The word's come down that the time to act is now. We've got search and seizure rights from the courts. Now's the time to break into that fortress, get the weapons and...get Koresh.

SUNDAY, FEBRUARY 27, 1993
8:30 a.m.

Our undercover agent reached a phone. His word is—NOW! If we can get in right away, Koresh and his followers won't have time to get to their weapons. ***If*** we can catch them by surprise.

9:30 a.m.

There's no sign of movement inside the fortress. We're a force of 100 highly-trained ATF agents. Many of us are hiding inside a smelly cattle trailer—a great front for us, but... There's the signal. We're moving in.

One group has reached the front. So far, so good. Their guns are aimed at the front door and at nearby windows. A second group has gone around back to get anyone who might try to escape. We've got to get the ladders up and scale the walls to see what Koresh has on the other side...

9:45 a.m.

SHOTS! That fool has machine guns! My, God! Pull back... We've got agents down... They're down!

A woman walks with her cross and two dogs near the Branch Davidian compound under siege by federal agents.

The Standoff Begins

10:00 a.m.

Retreat is ordered. Some are backing away—still firing at the fortress to cover themselves. One National Guard helicopter was forced down. It landed safely in a nearby field. A second chopper was ordered away.

10:15 a.m.

Agents are now in communication with Koresh. Both sides have agreed to a "cease fire." A "cease fire..." This is like being in the middle of a war!

10:20 a.m.

Bullet-proof shields have been distributed. We're going out to help the wounded—and retrieve the dead. Three cult members captured during the gunfight are now on their way to the local jail. They're facing charges of use of a firearm during commission of a violent crime and conspiracy to murder federal agents. If convicted, they could face the death penalty. Still, that's only three. The real man we want is still inside—alive and well.

10:30 a.m.

Koresh was waiting for us. Somehow he had to know! Just as our teams surrounded the place, cult members began firing. The most deadly gunfire came from the guard tower in the center of the compound. The cult members have a huge 50-millimeter machine gun up there. Its bullets can slice through body armor like a knife through hot butter. We simply weren't prepared for that kind of attack. We weren't even given a chance to fall back. The count so far: Four dead, 16 wounded. Now Koresh can add the charge of 1st degree murder to his list of criminal offenses. What does he hope to accomplish? Doesn't he know that he's endangering the lives of all those families and their children?

Afternoon

More agents and local police are pouring into the area to help surround the fortress. Two cult members tried to escape by shooting their way out, but they were shot and killed by return fire. This time we got them before they got us. The news media is having a time with this one. I wonder if they realize how much danger they're in as well?

7:30 p.m.

The scoop is that Koresh received a phone call at 8:40 a.m., warning him that we were coming. It's as we suspected—he knew we were coming!

Agents have been negotiating with Koresh all day, trying to get him to send out the children.

8:00 p.m.

Four children have left the fortress. Simple questioning indicates that six cult members were killed and several wounded, including Koresh himself. If he's really hurt, perhaps he'll give himself up.

MONDAY, MARCH 1, 1993
10:30 a.m.

Six more children have been released. This could be a sign that Koresh and the rest of the cult members will surrender peacefully. Still, the situation is unstable enough that we've brought in eight troop carriers. Heavily armed, these vehicles will protect us against any further attacks from the compound.

TUESDAY, MARCH 2, 1993
8:00 a.m.

Word of the failed attack has spread around the world. The place is crawling with reporters, cameramen and photographers. Everyone now knows the tragic beginning. Now the question is, How will this standoff end?

9:30 a.m.

Eight children and two elderly women were allowed to leave today. The women were sent as messengers, carrying with them a 58-minute tape that Koresh had recorded earlier today. It is being listened to and analyzed now.

10:45 a.m.

The message appears to be a somewhat "twisted" collection of Bible verses mixed with Koresh's ideas and beliefs. *But* the important part of this is that he has agreed to give himself up if radio and TV stations will broadcast this recording. We're working on that now. A peaceful end to this situation is more than any of us had hoped for.

1:30 p.m.

The Koresh tape is being played at a nearby station in Dallas. Media from around the world are picking it up, and sending it across the airwaves. Koresh should be pleased. We've got three buses in place outside the fortress. As soon as the Branch Davidians come out, they'll be immediately arrested.

A young child rides to safety in the back of an ATF van after being let go from the Branch Davidian cult compound.

11:00 p.m.

It's late. The buses remain empty. Koresh has gone back on his word and refuses to come out. I knew it was too good to be true.

The FBI has now taken over control of the situation. All totaled, there are more than 400 law enforcement officials here. Let's hope we all walk away from this confrontation alive.

WEDNESDAY, MARCH 3, 1993

8:00 a.m.

The FBI has now taken over communications with Koresh. They have asked him why he did not surrender as promised. Koresh indicated that he would not budge until God provides him with instructions for surrender. Now we have to wonder what kind of instructions Koresh will "hear."

9:00 a.m.

FBI field commander Bob Ricks has indicated that there will be no direct attack on the fortress. The risk is much too great for the 24 children and more than 80 adults inside. The plan now is to let Koresh wait... and wait... and wait. Sooner or later, he'll grow tired of his self-made prison. We can only hope that it will be sooner.

10:00 a.m.

Theories are now coming forward as to the security leak that forewarned Koresh of our raid. Ricks believes the informer may have been our own spy. We think it could have been one of the journalists who rode along with us that morning. It's unsettling wondering who was the snitch. Who can we trust, if not each other?

THURSDAY, MARCH 4, 1993
3:00 p.m.

For some unknown reason, Koresh released a 14-year-old boy and his 11-year-old brother today. Two more are safe.

Routine coverage of the area has now uncovered the body of a male cult member some 350 yards from the back of the fortress. He must have died during the February 28th attack. Another life senselessly lost.

FRIDAY MARCH 5, 1993
5:00 p.m.

Again, for unknown reasons, another child was released today.

The word is that the cult members are trying to make life as normal as possible for themselves inside the fortress while they wait for their leader to act one way or the other. FBI surveillance teams state that the cult members continue doing chores, washing clothes, etc. Life goes on.

We've made no move because Ricks fears that Koresh may order his followers to kill themselves if it looks like the agents are about to close in and arrest them. Koresh has such power over these people that they would willingly die if he told them to do so.

The Tanks Are Brought In

SUNDAY, MARCH 9, 1993
7:30 a.m.

Ricks has been talking to Koresh on the phone since before sun-up, and things are not going well. Koresh is becoming more and more angry. He's been trying to drive away the FBI by playing rock 'n roll music at an ear-splitting volume over giant speakers aimed over the fortress walls. Let's just say, it's not working.

MONDAY, MARCH 10, 1993
7:30 a.m.

Investigations indicate that there may be some storage sheds five miles from here that hold weapons and explosives belonging to the Branch Davidians. FBI agents have been dispatched to follow up on the lead.

8:30 a.m.

The lead was disappointing. The only things found were a few boxes of legally purchased shotgun shells.

10:00 a.m.

Koresh is becoming more unstable. He claims that he's ready for war, and has threatened to "blow those armored troop carriers 50 feet into the sky" if we approach the fortress. The cult members have also taken up positions in the windows—many armed with machine guns. No shots have been fired... yet.

2:30 p.m.

Ricks has ordered in four M-60 tanks. It's creating quite a stir among the civilians. The tanks look fearsome, but there are no "weapons" aboard. However, each tank is equipped with a 12-foot-long mechanical arm. With this type of equipment, we can use the arm to knock down walls, then pump tear gas into the compound. As part of my training program, I had to breathe that stuff. I know the effects it has on a person. At first it's just a burning feeling. Your eyes water. You're uncomfortable. Then you start to choke. And all you want to do is get out into the fresh air. There are no lasting effects, but when you're going through it, it's awful! With the M-60s we could fill an entire room with tear gas in less than 15 seconds. The Davidians would be overcome with the fumes before they could start shooting. It's a way to protect them and us. It's a plan.

A law enforcement official watches as an armored personnel carrier is deployed from the command center in Waco, Texas.

FRIDAY, MARCH 12, 1993
5:00 p.m.

Two more cult members were release by Koresh. Two more free. Two more safe.

SATURDAY, MARCH 13, 1993
3:00 p.m.

Communications inside the compound indicate that some of the injured cultists' wounds have become infected. They have no doctors inside. If an infection spreads throughout a body, it can kill.

SUNDAY, MARCH 14, 1993
7:50 p.m.

What's good for the goose is good for the gander, I guess. This time, the FBI has started playing loud music, with speakers pointed toward the compound. In addition, they've rigged up huge spotlights to shine on the fortress. By keeping the cult members awake night after night, we hope they'll become irritated enough to turn on Koresh. This combination of babies crying, whistles blowing and Tibetan monks chanting ought to get on people's nerves quick enough!

FRIDAY, MARCH 19, 1993
5:30 p.m.

The lights and music are not having any effect. Koresh and his followers are as determined as ever to stay inside the fortress. However, two men who wanted to leave before the music and lights started were allowed by Koresh to go.

Preparing for Battle

SUNDAY, MARCH 21, 1993
4:00 p.m.

Every day for the past week we've been moving in closer and closer. Each time we make a move, we have to take out some of the cult members' barriers—everything from old, junked cars to 55-gallon (208–liter) drums of diesel fuel and gasoline. These were particularly dangerous. One shot from the fortress and the gas would have exploded like a bomb.

A spotlight shines over the compound in the early morning hours.

Meanwhile, seven more adults surrendered. Ricks believes this is a positive sign. Maybe the stand-off is about to end.

THURSDAY, MARCH 25, 1993
4:50 p.m.

Today, someone escaped *into* the fortress. Apparently, a 25-year-old Houston man, who had been watching news reports of the crisis, slipped through our lines and ran up to the fortress. Koresh has apparently taken him in as a new follower. We just weren't expecting someone to sneak into the fortress!

SATURDAY, MARCH 27, 1993
7:00 p.m.

This is getting tiresome. Another man got through our lines and went into Koresh's compound!

SUNDAY, MARCH 28, 1993
6:00 p.m.

Reports confirm that Koresh is trying to convince his followers to kill themselves in the event he dies—either by his own hand or by one of our bullets. This is a time to worry.

TUESDAY, MARCH 30, 1993
7:00 p.m.

Dick DeGuerin, a criminal defense attorney from Houston, entered the compound today in the hopes that he could convince Koresh to surrender. He is assuring Koresh that both he and all the cult members will have nothing to fear from us if they give up now.

FRIDAY, APRIL 2, 1993
5:05 p.m.
Bad news. DeGuerin was not able to make Koresh surrender. We've stopped talking to him. Right now it seems as though he's just playing games with us.

SUNDAY, APRIL 4, 1993
Tomorrow at sundown is the start of the Jewish feast of Passover. The Branch Davidians believe God speaks to them during Passover. DeGuerin, after talking to Koresh today, believes that Koresh will surrender at the end of the Passover Holiday. Koresh is expecting a sign from God as to what to do. However, Koresh has also told cult members that this Passover would be the last they ever celebrate together. I wonder (and dread) what Koresh meant by that.

MONDAY, APRIL 12, 1993
Sunset
The feast of Passover ended minutes ago. We again positioned buses in front of the fortress. No one came out. Koresh is not surrendering.

TUESDAY, APRIL 13, 1993
DeGuerin has stated that Koresh is still waiting for a sign from God. What does he want? An earthquake? A volcano erupting? What needs to happen to get those people out of there?

Pumping In Tear Gas

FRIDAY, APRIL 16, 1993

Apparently there's been no sign from God, because Koresh isn't doing anything. Ricks said today that if the cult leader does not give up soon, we'll have to act. Keeping this cult headquarters surrounded with personnel has now reached close to $50 million! It can't go on forever. No one wants it to.

SUNDAY, APRIL 18, 1993

We've cleared away nearly all the junk cars from around the fortress. The FBI's troop carriers and tanks have gotten their closest yet to the cult's borders.

MONDAY, APRIL 19, 1993
5:30 a.m.

The time for action has finally arrived. We've dispatched state troopers to homes in the immediate area, warning civilian personnel to stay inside for the next few hours. To avoid any further chance of leaks, no additional information is being given out, just a warning to expect a lot of noise.

5:50 a.m.

One last call has been made to Koresh: "Come out with your hands up now or we're coming in to get you." He responded by having someone toss the telephone out the front door. Clearly Koresh will not surrender.

6:04 a.m.
One of the M-60s is moving into position. It's there, at the fortress wall. *CRASH!* The battering ram has smashed a huge hole in the fortress wall to the left of the front door. I can hear the crackle of gunfire coming from inside. This is not going to be simple, nor safe.

6:20 a.m.
The tank is backing up for a second jab at the fortress. Bullets are flying everywhere!

8:00 a.m.
Over and over, the M-60 has bashed holes in the wall, stopping only long enough to pump tear gas into the exposed rooms. A second tank has moved into position at the rear of the fortress. Ricks has told us that as soon as the walls are knocked down, the tanks will drive into the middle of the fortress. Their next objective will be to chip away at the concrete bunker where Koresh and most of his followers are probably hiding.

9:00 a.m.
President Clinton has just addressed the nation, lending his support to Attorney General Janet Reno. As head of the FBI, it was under her authority that this plan of action received the "go ahead."

11:30 a.m.
The fortress has been flooded with tear gas. What's odd is that no one has tried to escape the painful fumes. The cult members may have gas masks, but these can protect them for only so long before they wear out and become useless. We should see cult members any time now...

The Compound Goes Up In Flames

12:05 p.m.

Smoke and flames are erupting from the fortress in three different areas! Something's gone wrong—dreadfully wrong. That gas shouldn't have started a fire. With the strong wind that's blowing, the fire is racing from building to building.

12:07 p.m.

Now the entire fortress is on fire! There's an explosion—a fireball just rocketed into the sky! If memory serves me, that explosion came from the area where Koresh's "throne room" is located.

12:20 p.m.

There's someone! One person, covered head-to-toe in soot, has just come out with his hands raised above his head. Wait... there's a few more coming out, too!

12:28 p.m.

Nine people. Nine lives out of 84 have come out of the smouldering remains of Koresh's complex. The blaze has consumed everything in it's path, and now there's little left to keep it going. As the flames burn themselves out and the smoke clears, we can see that the entire compound is a blackened mound of ash. There is little hope that anyone inside could have survived such an inferno.

12:40 p.m.

Fire trucks have just arrived. It's too late. The compound and the 86 men, women, and children inside are gone. The only thing left in that mournful setting is a blue-and-white Star of David flag flying on a pole above the fortress.

1:00 p.m.

The stand-off is officially over, but now we have to find the answers to a number of questions. Why didn't more of the cult members try to escape the tear gas and the fire? How did the fire start? Should we have used another plan to capture Koresh and his people? Should we have just kept waiting? With so many lives lost, the answers are not going to come easy. Not for any of us involved in this disaster!

Fire engulfs the Branch Davidian compound after FBI agents smashed the buildings with tanks and pumped in tear gas. The Justice Department said cult members set the fire.

Epilogue: Lessons To Be Learned

TUESDAY
APRIL 20, 1993

The grisly search through the charred rubble begins today. As we search for bodies, we're also desperately looking for clues that will help answer our questions.

Cyrus and Star Koresh, two of the many innocent children who lost their lives in the Waco tragedy.

THURSDAY
APRIL 22, 1993
8:00 a.m.

Attorney General Janet Reno has been called before Congress to explain what happened here. She explained that the FBI moved forward with the attack on April 19th because there was evidence that Koresh was hurting the 24 children who were inside with him. She also noted that the attack was very carefully planned even though it certainly did not end the way it was supposed to. As for the fire, cult members acting on Koresh's order started it.

MAY 1993

Medical examiners believe that some of the cult members died not from the fire, but from gunshot wounds. It is a possibility that Koresh shot his own people to prevent them from leaving and to scare the rest of them into perishing with him in the flames. Koresh's body was found off by itself in his "throne room."

The strange thing is that Koresh proved himself right about one thing: He always predicted the world would end in fire. His world did. Sadly, he took with him many innocent people.

The Waco disaster taught us a hard lesson. It reminded us of the frightening power one person can hold over others. This tragedy shows that we must stay on guard against power that overwhelms good judgement. Perhaps the Waco tragedy will help to prevent another day of disaster.

Aerial view of the charred remains of the Branch Davidian compound.

Index